PENGUIN BOOKS

IT NEVER RAINS

Roger McGough was born in Liverpool, and received the Freedom of the City in 2001. During the 1960s he was a member of the group Scaffold, which had an international hit with 'Lily the Pink'. He presents the popular Radio 4 programme *Poetry Please*, and is President of the Poetry Society. He has published many books of poems for adults and children, most recently *As Far As I Know* (Viking, 2012), and both his *Collected Poems* (2003) and his *Selected Poems* (2006) are available in Penguin. His trio of Molière translations – *Tartuffe*, *The Hypochondriac* and *The Misanthrope* – have been notable successes recently in the theatre. In 2005 he received a CBE for services to literature.

'Home James and don't spare the Norses'

It Never Rains

Roger McGough

PENGUIN BOOKS

PENGUIN BOOKS

Published by the Penguin Group
Penguin Books Ltd, 80 Strand, London WC2R 0RL, England
Penguin Group (USA) Inc., 375 Hudson Street, New York, New York 10014, USA
Penguin Group (Canada), 90 Eglinton Avenue East, Suite 700, Toronto, Ontario, Canada M4P 2Y3
(a division of Pearson Penguin Canada Inc.)
Penguin Ireland, 25 St Stephen's Green, Dublin 2, Ireland (a division of Penguin Books Ltd)
Penguin Group (Australia), 707 Collins Street, Melbourne, Victoria 3008, Australia
(a division of Pearson Australia Group Pty Ltd)
Penguin Books India Pvt Ltd, 11 Community Centre, Panchsheel Park, New Delhi – 110 017, India
Penguin Group (NZ), 67 Apollo Drive, Rosedale, Auckland 0632, New Zealand
(a division of Pearson New Zealand Ltd)
Penguin Books (South Africa) (Pty) Ltd, Block D, Rosebank Office Park, 181 Jan Smuts Avenue,
Parktown North, Gauteng 2193, South Africa

Penguin Books Ltd, Registered Offices: 80 Strand, London WC2R 0RL, England

www.penguin.com

This collection published 2014
001

Copyright © Roger McGough, 2014

The moral right of the author has been asserted

Text Design by Claire Mason
Typeset by Penguin Books
Printed in Great Britain by Clays Ltd, St Ives plc

A CIP catalogue record for this book is available from the British Library

ISBN: 978-0-241-97142-0

www.greenpenguin.co.uk

Penguin Books is committed to a sustainable
future for our business, our readers and our
planet. This book is made from paper certified
by the Forest Stewardship Council.

Contents

Erratum

For *'heaving'* in line one read *'heaven'*
For *'one'* in line one read *'eleven'*
For *'tomato'* in line seven read *'a martyr'*
For *'Erratum'* in title read *'Errata'*.

The Once-Empty Page

This page was empty
Its mind was blank
It used to gaze out vacantly
And thank the lord
The written word
Had given it a miss

And then this.

And this

And this

nd this

and this and this and this and this

It never rains but it.....

Skywriting

Clouds are the earth's handwriting.
I open the sky
And don't like what I'm reading.

In Good Spirits

This icy winter's morning I rise in good spirits.
On all fours I exhale a long white breath
That hangs in the air like a shimmering rope
Under which, with arms akimbo
And eyes ablaze, I dance the limbo.

Ex Patria

After supper, we move out on the veranda.
Moths flit between lamps. We drink, think about sex
and consider how best to wreck each other's lives.

At the river's edge, the kitchen maids are washing up.
In the age-old tradition, they slap the plates
against the side of a rock, singing tonelessly.

Like tiny chauffeurs, the mosquitoes will soon arrive
and drive us home. O England, how I miss you.
Ascot, Henley, Wimbledon. It's the little things.

Mensa

'His parents knew he was brighter than most other children, when
Joshua potty-trained himself at 23 months after reading
a book on the subject.' – *Daily Telegraph*

Yes, Josh was the brightest by far
Posh, bookish and swotty
Six 'A's at thirteen, each with a star
Went up to Cambridge. Took his potty.

Oxbridge Blues

While up at Magdalen
Spent the time dagdalen.

Moved on to Caius
Became the baius knaius.

Half-term

Half-term holiday, family away
Half-wanting to go, half-wanting to stay
Stay in bed for half the day.

Half-read, half-listen to the radio
Half-think things through. Get up,
Half-dressed, half-wonder what to do.

Eat half a loaf, drink half a bottle
(Save the other half until later).
Other half rings up. Feel better.

Away from You

Away from you
I feel a great emptiness
a gnawing loneliness

With you
I get that reassuring feeling
of wanting to escape.

Good Old William

'I concur with everything you say,'
smiled William.

'Oh yes, I concur with that,
I agree.'

'If that's the general feeling you can count on me.
Can't say fairer.'

Good old
William, the Concurrer.

it suits you

Writer's Block

The excitement I felt
as I started the poem
Disappeared on reaching
the end of the fourth line.

Executioner's Block

Money good
Hours short
Can't stand blood
Don't like sport

Had to stop
Nervous wreck
Given chop
Pain in neck.

Children's Writer

John in the garden
Playing goodies and baddies

Janet in the bedroom
Playing mummies and daddies

Mummy in the kitchen
Washing and wiping

Daddy in the study
Stereotyping.

For Want of a Better Title

The Countess
when the Count passed away

During a Bach
cello recital

Married an Archduke
the following day

For want of a better title.

The State of Poetry

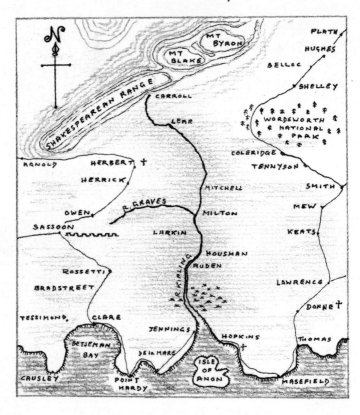

New Poem

So far, so good

Sound Advice

Once you write a poem
you must write another

To prevent the first
from falling over.

Riddle

To ease us
through those difficult days

At hand to tease out
waifs and strays

Though causing pain
we squeeze you again

and again. Vain? Not really
more a fear of the unruly

If you wish to borrow mine
simply repeat the opening line.

Literary Riddle

I am
Out of my tree
Away with the fairies
A nut. A fruitcake. What am I?

Answers: Tweezers.
One line short of a cinquain.

Acrostic

A favourite literary devi
Ce is the one whe
Re the first letter
Of each line spell
S out the subject the poe
T wishes to write about.
I must admit, I
Can't see the point myself.

Non secateurs

Granny's Favourite Anagram

A granma
is an anagram
of anagram.

Clerihews

Jane Austen
Got lost in
Stoke-on-Trent.
Moral: She shouldn't have went.

Edmund Clerihew Bentley
Invented the *clerihew* accidentally.
And incidentally,
Why didn't he call it the *bentley*?

Clara Hughes
Invented *clarahughes*
'After me they're named,'
She claimed.

What do you think of my new Clerihew?
Very nice Bentley.

Apostrophe

What fun to be
an apostrophe
floating above an s
Hovering like a paper kite
in between the its
Eavesdropping, tiptoeing
high above the thats
An inky comet spiralling
The highest tossed of hats.

A Critic Reviews the Curate's Egg

'It's all bad.
Especially in parts.'

@thomasdylan LOL

*'What Dylan Thomas means to me in 140 characters –
bringing him into the modern era in the form of a text'*
                                    Request from the *Western Mail*

He fell in love with words as a child
Language-guzzler, dazzling, wild.
Crazily obscure, lyrical yet tough
To describe the magic, one hundred
And forty characters is not enou

Epitaphs

The Wreck of the Hesperus

A lass
bound to a mast
drowned
alas.

Lady Godiva

Here lies Lady Godiva.
She didn't wear a bra
or knickers iva.

Moll Flanders

Here lies Moll Flanders.
It has to be said
a thief, a whore
and five times wed.

Adept was she
at social climbing
then repented.
Nice timing.

The After-Dinner Speaker

Sitting around the table each evening
his wife and children pick nervously
at their food, dreading the sound
of the tapping of the knife against the glass,
of the rapping of the spoon upon the table,
signalling that he will rise to his feet
and upstanding, speak for forty minutes.
An hour sometimes, if the wine kicks in.

How they look forward to those nights when he's away,
at a conference, say, of managers or teachers.
And they don't have to listen
To those boring, yawning after-dinner speeches.

The Perfect Crime

The sword-swallower
stabbed his unfaithful
wife to death

Before disposing
of the murder weapon
in one gulp.

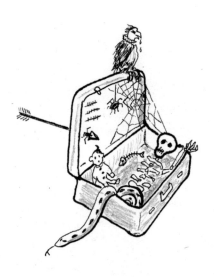

Worst case scenario

Drop Dead Gorgeous

Inserting a deadly comma into the cliché
He said, 'Drop dead, gorgeous,'
Then pulled the trigger

Whoops!

You are strangely excited
as we enter the crowded bar
and find a small table in the corner.

You insist on fetching the drinks
and before disappearing
squeeze a note into my hand.

It reads: 'Why go home tonight?
I have a room. I have a bed.
I have a spare toothbrush.'

I recognize my own handwriting.

Deadpan Delivery

I was popping a few frozen
Fugo fish fingers under the grill
When there came a loud knocking

Quickly donning my clown costume,
I opened the door.
It was the Deadpan Man with a delivery

'Do I have to sign for this?' I asked.
'No, I'm not hard of hearing,'
He quipped, deadpan.

Sign Language

Hannah said that at boarding school
Talking in the dorm was forbidden after lights out
So she and her friends devised a form of sign language.
Trouble was, in the dark, they couldn't see what they were saying.

The Juggler

Cousin Amos, famous in his day
Would only juggle with objects
Beginning with 'A'

Like Acorns, Apples and Anchovies
Alarm clocks, Armadillos and Armchairs
And just the once, an Alligator

Which, sad to say
Went straight for the jugular.

Fame

The best thing
about being famous

is when you walk
down the street

and people turn round
to look at you

and bump into things.

Vanity Press

Fell in love with my editor
wrote poems, yearned for her lips

She married a literary critic
now sends me rejection slips.

Q

I join the queue
We move up slowly.

'What are we queuing for?'
I ask the lady in front of me.
'To join another queue,' she explains.
'How pointless,' I say, 'I'm leaving.'
She points to another long queue
'Then you must get in line.'

I join the queue
We move up slowly.

You Asked For a Poem

You asked for a poem
off the top of my head
I plucked out a hair
'That's not fair' you said.

Rhyming Sausages

(i)

Sausages though tasty
Are difficult to rhyme.
Unlike pies
Which rhyme with *skies* for instance.
And *lies*, and *surprise* and *sighs*
And *capsize* and *flies* and *prize*.
To mention only seven.

(ii)

Sausages though tasty
Are difficult to rhyme.
Unlike a pasty
Which rhymes with *nasty*.
Oddly, it doesn't rhyme with tasty.

(iii)

Sausages though tasty
Are difficult to rhyme
So I seldom eat them.

The Rhyming Diner

Dear waiter,

I'm sorry but the service was poor.
I'm not being picky
But the cutlery was sticky
And the soup ended up on the floor.

The stew was too gooey
The chicken too chewy
And yuck! That frozen chip.

So enough's enough
I'm off in a huff
Here's a poem instead of a tip.

'cat got your tongue has it?'

Shearing on the Côte d'Azur

In playful homage to the summer jazz festival
a topiarized bush in the shape of a grand piano
stands on a roundabout outside Vence

Every Sunday morning, a blind musician
with green fingers, sits at the keyboard
and with a pair of garden shears, tunes it.

Jellyfish Morton

This morning out walking I saw
A jellyfish playing piano on the shore

The hottest jazz, the coolest blues
I started to dance in my shiny shoes

'What's your name?' I asked
When he stopped for tea

'Jellyfish Morton,' he said
'And you can take it from me
It don't mean a thing if it ain't got no sting.'
Then he slipped back into the sea.

A Good Age

On reaching a good age
She died

The years before
Had all been bad

Then she reached a good age
and died. How sad. How sad.

Invisible mender

Rubber Bullets

They sound harmless but without a doubt
Rubber bullets rub people out

VAT

I do not value
Added tax

Windows of the Soul

If eyes are the windows of the soul
Are eyelids the window cleaners?

There are fascists

There are fascists
pretending
to be humanitarian

        like cannibals
        on a health kick
        eating only
        vegetarians.

Conservative Government Unemployment Figures

Conservative Government.
Unemployment?
Figures.

The Leader

I wanna be the leader
I wanna be the leader
Can I be the leader?
Can I? I can?
Promise? Promise?
Yippee, I'm the leader
I'm the leader.

OK what shall we do?

A Brush with Authority

I had a brush with authority
Not only did it tell me
What to paint, but also
Which colours to use

Uncle Eno

To be a sumo wrestler it pays to be fat
'Nonsense,' said Eno, 'I don't believe that.'

So he took his skinny, little frame
To Tokyo in search of fame

But even with God on his side
Eno got trod on, and died.

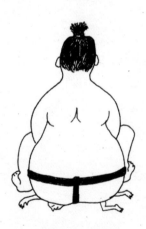

Uncle Malcolm

Uncle Malcolm put the shot for Scotland.
When he retired he collected shots as a hobby

At the time of his death he had nearly 200
And in accordance with his last wishes

They were buried with him at St Giles' Cemetery in Perth
Uncle Mal is now at rest, somewhere near the centre of the earth.

Uncle Pat

Going into bat against the Windies
in his first (and final) Test
Uncle Pat wore vinyl undies
and an armour-plated vest.

But in the panic to get dressed
(wickets falling thick and fast)
left his box off.

Third ball took his rocks off.

Uncle Jed

Uncle Jed, Durham bred,
raced pigeons for money.

He died a poor man however,
as the pigeons were invariably
too quick for him.

Cousin Nell

Cousin Nell married a frogman
in the hope that one day
he would turn into a handsome prince.

Instead,
he turned into a sewage pipe near Gravesend
and was never seen again.

Cousin Daisy

Cousin Daisy's
favourite sport
was standing
on streetcorners.

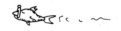

She contracted
with ease
a funny disease.
Notwithstanding.

Hill of Beans

'Life ain't nuttin' but a hill o' beans,'
drawled Granma, and removing
her corncob pipe, spat a stream
of baccy juice into the empty firegrate
before settling back with a jug of bourbon
into her old rocking chair.

To think, only this time last year
she was working for the Welsh Water Authority.

Granny

Granny plays whist
better when pwhist.

Quick on the Draw

He was so quickonthedraw
he fired twice
had a haircut
a drink in the saloon
and rode out of town
before the sheriff's hand
hit the holster.

Slow on the Drawl

'Howdy y'all'
said the Texan
(slow on the drawl).

Gun Love

After the outlaw had bitten the dust
Never again to rise

The sheriff takes you for a spin round his finger
Then blows the smoke from your eyes.

Moist

Oiled and snug
In a moist holster

Six deadly pearls
In a gross oyster.

Poem on the Underground

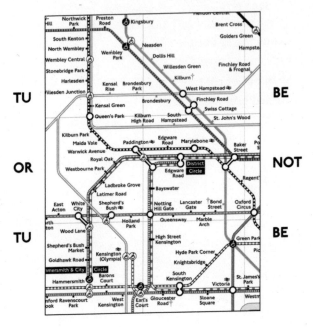

Concourse

Lonely on a crowded concourse?
Don't grow cantankerous
Somebody loves you
Here at St Pancras.

Ode to the Leaf
(*Nissan's zero-emission electric car*)

Cornering too fast
He came to grief
Spun out of control
Turned over a new Leaf.

Autosuggestion

My wife keeps hinting
It's time we had a new car.
Autosuggestion.

Hippoposthumous

Recycling

I care about the environment
And try to do what is right
So I cycle to work every morning
And recycle home every night.

Survivor

Everyday
I think about dying.
About disease, starvation,
violence, terrorism, war,
the end of the world.

It helps keep my mind off things.

Multi-Storey Car Park

If multi-storey car parks could talk
What stories they could tell
About cars, petrol and parking
But they can't, which is just as well.

Multi-Storey Carp Ark

Five Ways to Help You Pass Safely through a Dark Wood Late at Night

1. Whistle a tune your father whistled when you were a child
2. Cross the first two fingers of your left hand
3. If you lose sight of the moon hold it in the mind's eye
4. Imagine the colours that surround you waiting for the first kiss of morning
5. Keep a Kalashnikov in the glove compartment.

Do I make myself plain?

Dear Scott

This is just to say
I have drunk
the plum brandy
that was in
the icebox

and which
you were probably
saving
for breakfast

Forgive me
it was delicious
so cold
and so numbing

x Zelda

My god Zelda, that wasn't brandy. it was a bottle I was using for . .

Drinking Song

Drink wine
Think romance
You're a lover

Feel fine
Sing and dance
Fall over.

Passive Drinking

Is passive drinking dangerous?
You'd think not, but last night
After watching a man down fourteen pints
I passed out like a light.

Missed

Out of work
divorced
usually pissed.

He aimed
low in life
and

       missed.

The Bright Side

Things are so bad
I am reduced to scraping
the outside of the barrel.

And yet, I do not despair.
In the yard there are many
worse off than myself. (Well, four:

A one-eyed rat
A three-legged cat
A corpse and the lavatory door.)

Hard Times

When we were up we were beaten
When we were down we were kicked
We used to be given meals-on-wheels
Until the wheels got nicked.

Depressed?

When you're
depressed
deep rest
is best.

7 a.m.

Alarm clock sends fire engines
Clanging into my nightmares

Bedroom is cold

Reach out and put on my hangover.

Somnambulance

Another Mid-Life Crisis

3 a.m. Feeling like death
and wanting to end it all
I reach for the paracetamol.
Will there be enough?

One by one I count them out. 72?
Need more to be on the safe side.
Rummaging around I add another 30.
That should do it.

Take the first two with a glass of water.
Feel better. Go back to bed. Fall asleep.

My Philosophy in a Nutshell

Nothing to hear, nothing to see
When will the nutcracker set me free?

Worry

Where would we be without worry?
It helps keep the brain occupied.
Doing doesn't take your mind off things,
I've tried.

Worry is God's gift to the nervous.
Best if kept bottled inside.
I once knew a man who couldn't care less.
He died.

Wartime Blues

Sex is rationed
and the dog has chewed
all the coupons.

Fired with Enthusiasm

This morning
the boss
came into work
bursting
with enthusiasm

and fired everybody.

Clock, watching

Early-Morning Poems

(i)

Got up
did my toilet:
Washed
Shaved
Combed hair

My toilet looks much nicer now.

(ii)

Got up
Had shave
Did *Times* crossword

Had another shave.

The State of the Bathroom

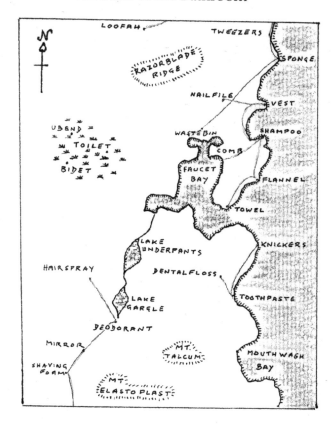

The lost Lost Property Office

'On buses and trains you wouldn't believe
The crazy things that passengers leave

A ventriloquist's dummy mouthing a scream
Two tickets (unused) for Midsummer Night's Dream

Handcuffs, chains and a spiderman suit
The tangled remains of a failed parachute

Rucksacks, tents and rolled-up beds
If they weren't screwed on they'd lose their heads

Two bull terriers and a Siamese kitten
Suicide note, hastily written

Garden forks with broken handles
A birthday cake with four candles

A file with TOP SECRET stamped in red
(Inside a card, *April Fool* it said)

Safe and secure behind a locked door
Priceless works of art by the score

Paintings by Hockney, Warhol and Blake
Two Mona Lisas (possibly fake)

Magritte's bowler hat and Van Gogh's chair
Duchamp's urinal and a paint-stained pair

Of trousers belonging to Toulouse Lautrec
(short in the leg, black and white check)

A painting by numbers of Rembrandt's head
Dirty sheet and a pillow off Tracey's bed

Jigsaw by Rodin, of two lovers kissing
Damien Hirst skull with the diamonds missing

Am I overworked? Of course I am
The list goes on ad nauseam

A shot putter's shot and a pole vaulter's pole
A partial eclipse and a Black Hole

A bucket of toenails and a wooden plank
Two air-to-air missiles and a Russian tank

The Statue of Liberty and an oil slick
Mountains of mobiles and an old walking stick

Lost any of these? Bad news I'm afraid
The Lost Property Office has been mislaid.'

The Wicked Queen's Mirror

Here she comes:
'**Mirror, mirror on the wall,**
who is the fairest of them all?'
One of these days, just for a joke
I'll say 'Dopey' and watch her choke.

The Cracked Mirror

It came as a shock
But I live in hope
A new life beckons
As a kaleidoscope.

Rear-View Mirror

It is difficult
To get a good view of your bottom
In a mirror

The Dental Mirror

How would you like to spend your days
Among yellowing tusks and grey tombstones?
Sloshing around in slimy tunnels
Dodging mashers and angry gnashers?
Tongues like skinned whales threshing
In whirlpools of blood and gunge?

Much rather work in a hairdressing salon
For people with miniature heads.

What Man Wears

What man wears beneath his trousers
Women confide, seldom arouses

Silken briefs or satin thong
Will make her giggle loud and long

Of course, you'll never stand a chance
in saggy, Y-front underpants

Wear boxer shorts, ideally plain
(Not Disney, cartoons are a pain

in the bum) Tartan only for the Scots
No stars and stripes, no polka dots

No union jacks or football logos
Phallic jokes? Definitely no-noes

Regard your underwear as a friendly go-between
So teach it manners, and above all, keep it clean.

Bath – Avon

I have a problem with Bath.
I use the short a, rhyming it with math,
Whereas southerners put in the r. Barth.

So my living there would be a kind of hell
(Although a lovely place by all accounts).
Never have an operation you cannot spell
Or live in a town you mispronounce.

Hen Party

Men seldom make passes
At girls who throw glasses

But may find romances
With those who throw glances.

HEAD ROOM

LEG ROOM

BED ROOM

STEAM ROOM

MUSIC ROOM

MUSH ROOM

TEA ROOM

63

BALL ROOM

Life is but a Tree

When the sky is closing in
And the future looks appalling
Remember life is but a tree
Medium-sized and falling.

When the Bough Breaks

When the bough breaks and you're falling
Enjoy one last look around
For Time, impatient, accelerates
The nearer you get to the ground.

In Good Hands

Wherever night falls
The earth is always
There to catch it.

Ring

Your finger
sadly
has a familiar ring
about it.

Love Cycle

Up against the wall
locked in passionate embrace
our two bicycles.

Cake

I wanted one life
you wanted another
we couldn't have our cake
so we ate eachother.

Friends of the Earth

Ecology Jim was a Friend of the Earth.
But the earth was no friend of Jim.
When living he covered all of it
Now it covers all of him.

Palmistry

Palmists in Polynesia
Read palm trees
Because it's easier.

Cane Toads

Please don't.

Rainforest Gateau

Too many cooks
Recipe gone wrong
Still on the menu
But not for long.

Fatal Consequences

I don't believe that one about the butterfly –
The air displaced by the fluttering
of its wings in Brazil
causing a tidal wave in Bangladesh.

Mind you,
The day after I shook out
a tablecloth on the patio
there was an earthquake in Mexico.

(Or was it the other way round?)

Global Warming

In the Antarctic, an ice-shelf
twice the size of Norfolk
has broken off, and is melting.

People the world over are concerned.
Especially those in Suffolk
who always get the thin end of the wedge.

Wiwis

To amuse
emus
on warm summer nights

Kiwis*
do wiwis
from spectacular heights.

Ostrich

One morning
an ostrich
buried his head
in the sand
and fell asleep

On waking
he couldn't remember
where he'd buried it.

** In the skies above New Zealand
Kiwis once abounded
But for health & safety reasons
For years now they've been grounded*

68

Seagulls

Seagulls are eagles
with no head for heights

For soggy old crusts
they get into fights

Out-of-tune buskers
beggars and screechers

Seagulls are not
my favourite creatures.

A 13-Amp Slug

A 13-amp slug
you are likely to find
in the garden under a rock

Be careful
how you pick it up

You might get
a nasty shock.

The Deserted Village
(After Oliver Goldsmith)

Sweet Auburn, loveliest village of the plain,
The new runway opens at Heathrow.
Hark! A jumbo jet.......and again...
And again...and again...and again...

Taking Stick

I may be a stick insect
But I'm not thin I'm thick

I married my childhood sweetheart
Who turned out to be a stick

Light Sleeper

My wife is such a light sleeper
that when I come home late
after a night out with the boys
I always remove my shoes
and leave them at the bottom
of the street.

Imagine my surprise, when
on retrieving them this morning
I discovered that they had been
polished.

What a nice neighbourhood I live in.
What a great country this is.

Neighbourhood Watch

It's a sin
It's a crime
Now we can't tell the time
Our neighbourhood watch
Has been stolen!

Fire Guard

My wife bought a fire guard for the living room.
Seems a nice sort of chap.

Poem against Capital Punishment

I live in the Capital
And it's punishment

The Concise Guide for Travellers

1) For covering long distances travel is a must.
2) Destinations are ideal places to head for.
3) By the time you get there abroad will have moved on.
4) To avoid jet lag travel the day before.
5) If you meet an explorer you are lost.

Ah, I see where you're coming from now

The Dada Christmas Catalogue

Star-bangled spanner
Chocolate comb
Can-of-worms opener
One book end
Solar-powered sun-bed
Abrasive partridges
Inflatable fridge
Set of nervous door handles
Overnight tea-bag
Instant coffee table
Sly trombone
Pair of cheapskates
Mobile phone-booth
Underwater ashtray
13 amp bath plug
Pair of socks, identical but for the colour
Another book end
Portable suitcase
Genetic make-up bag
Demystifying spray
Packet of party-poopers
Box of (past their sell-by) dates
Nasal floss (unwaxed)

Contact lens adhesive
Magnetic chopsticks
Concrete poetry-mixer
Non-secateurs
Not a pipe.

Punk doll

Last week
I bought my favourite niece
a cute little doll
from a punk toy shop
in the King's Road.

When you twist the safety pin
in her rosy cheek
she vomits and shouts
'shitshitshitshitshit'
in a tinny voice.

The doll is pretty strange too.

Lonely Hearts

(i)
Hiawatha, feeling randy
on the shores of Gitche-gumme
Thinking squaw would come in handy
to scritchy-scratchy itchy tummy

Plenty big-bam in the wigwam
where the laughing waters flow
Fire an arrow, make me quiver
Minnehaha ho ho ho.

(ii)
Pied Piper
(kids flown the nest)
seeks lady piper
(preferably undressed)

for reels and jigs
and entrechats.
Do not apply
unless fond of rats.

(iii)
Matilda
(who told such dreadful lies)
seeks handsome fireman
with coal-black eyes
and huge moustache on,
to set her alight
and quench her passion.

(iv)
To whit-
owl owner of peagreen boat
seeks pussy-cat
for low jinks
on high seas
-*To woo!*

Weight-Watching

'Dear Lonely Hearts, my name is Nate,
My hobbies are weightlifting and tempting fate'

'Dear Nate, my name is Kate,
My hobby is weight-watching, please name the date'

He showered her with gifts
Now Kate watches as Nate lifts.

Scintillate

I have outlived
my youthfulness
so a quiet life for me.

Where once
I used to
scintillate

now I sin
till ten
past three.

VROOM- ROOM

italic

ONCE I LIVED IN CAPITALS
MY LIFE INTENSELY PHALLIC

but now i'm sadly lowercase
with the occasional *italic*.

Friends, Flies and Fingernails

Those I grow old with

Dropping like them

Clinging on by them

Dressed for the Occasion

I have enough sweaters and trousers
Though shirts I may need to replace
A couple of suits I can Oxfam
As they take up far too much space

One overcoat, one jacket, leather
One linen suit for summer weather
Hats, of course, and a dressing-gown
Should last until the blind comes down.

Time Flies

We're led to believe
But it's us that fly
Time sits on its hands
As we rush by

Said and Done

When all's said and done
There'll be nothing left to say or do.

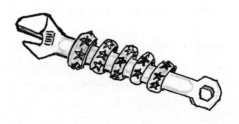

star bangled spanner

The Proverbials

You can't toboggan on a level playing-field

Even Big Bad Wolves have nightmares

The bigger the wooden clog, the smaller the forest

The surgeon removed a warm cockle from her heart

Mice that live with stay-at-home cats, seldom play

Lost, the navigator circled the square in search of a compass

The air was foul until a frank discussion cleared it

The jogger ran up some debts, and then down some

The scales fell from her eyes, badly bruising her toes

Why is the graffiti always neater on the other side of the stairwell?

Prozac provides safety in numbness

Is a dartboard an objet d'art?

Married men live longer than single men.
    Or does it just seem that way?

Writing novels is outside my jurisfiction

Why do playwrights always have to dramatize everything?

'Shy poet seeks post as Writer-in-Reticence'

The lovers warmed their hands in the heat of the moment

A suitcase becomes heavy only when lifted

In summer as hot air rises, so the days get lighter

If you want to put the clock back,
    simply clear a space on the mantlepiece

Had the shield been invented first,
    would the sword have been thought of?

Some eggs are not sure they are eggs

Table mats are for wiping your feet before dancing on tables

Toilet rolls are the somersaults that toilets make
    when tossed into a skip

The rubber ring lacked a certain je ne sais quoit

To achieve wisdom, arrive after the event

Every journey is an epic

Lost in the desert, the interior designer quickly went insane

When I was at school, teachers used the carrot and stick
method of education. Without the carrot.

In dusty cupboards, teachers' canes spend the
years wondering what they did wrong

The square of the hypotenuse was filled with buskers
and mime artists

Revenge, unlike Lancashire hot-pot, is a dish best served cold

It may fizz with bubbles but it's still water

Still waters run deep, although not in saucers

He is so shy he even stammers when he's thinking

When one glove is missing, both are lost

Having smashed the hand mirror,
the princess could no longer admire her hands

A: The answer

Q: Which came first, the question or the answer?

Questions have a lot to answer for

To claim the reward, one must hand over the kitten

What fun times chameleons have on zebra crossings

Water boils only when the bubbles tell it to

Old people do not walk slowly because they have plenty of time

My shadow is but a shadow of its former self

The book stops here.